Extreme Cars

RACE CARS

Steve Rendle

PowerKiDS press.

New York

Published in 2022 by The Rosen Publishing Group, Inc.
29 East 21st Street, New York, NY 10010

Cataloging-in-Publication Data

Names: Rendle, Steve.
Title: Hypercars / Steve Rendle.
Description: New York : PowerKids Press, 2022. | Series: Extreme cars | Includes glossary and index.
Identifiers: ISBN 9781725332416 (pbk.) | ISBN 9781725332430 (library bound) | ISBN 9781725332423 (6 pack) | ISBN 9781725332447 (ebook)
Subjects: LCSH: Sports cars--Juvenile literature.
Classification: LCC TL236.R448 2022 | DDC 629.228--dc23

Design by Richard Parsons and James Robertson

The following agencies have given permission to use their images:

Photographs supplied by the individual car manufacturers.
Additional images published with the permission of Getty.
Cover, tcharts/Shutterstock.com; Cover, p. 1 Double Brain/Shutterstock.com; pp. 3-5, 8, 9, 12, 13, 16, 17, 20, 21, 24, 25, 28-32 Carlos Caetano/Shutterstock.com.

Manufactured in the United States of America

CPSIA Compliance Information: Batch #CWPK22. For Further Information contact Rosen Publishing, New York, New York at 1-800-237-9932.

CONTENTS

INTRODUCTION

This book is about race cars, and we've picked some of the most extreme ones in the world. You might wonder what made us select some but not others. Well, for a start, all the cars in this book have been, or will be, available to buy, as long as buyers have enough money and, in some cases, if they meet the conditions that the car manufacturer sets. You won't see these cars every day—and there are some that you will probably never see—but they are all out there on the world's roads or tracks somewhere!

Most of the cars are very modern and fitted with the latest technology. There are a few older cars too. However old they are, though, all the cars included have been selected because they are built to provide an incredible experience for the driver—but not necessarily for passengers. In most cases, the cars need a skilled driver to make the most of them. Some are racing cars for the road, while others are road cars that were built so that they could also be raced.

Every one of the cars included has extreme performance—either top speed or acceleration—and most are able to corner like racing cars. Of course, they all sound incredible. Some have road-car luxuries too, such as leather trim, in-car entertainment, air conditioning, and satnav.

Perhaps one day you might be lucky enough to get behind the wheel of one of the ultimate machines featured in the following pages and find out just how exciting they can be. Until then, enjoy reading and daydreaming about them!

ABBREVIATIONS AND THEIR MEANINGS

bhp	brake horsepower—available power of an engine
cc	cubic centimeters—volume of engine cylinders added together
in	inches—used for wheel sizes
kg	kilograms—unit of weight
kph	kilometers per hour—unit of speed
kW	kilowatts—unit of power
lb	pounds—unit of weight
lb ft	pound foot—unit of torque
LCD	liquid-crystal display
mm	millimeters—unit of length
mph	miles per hour—unit of speed
Nm	newton meter—unit of torque
rpm	revolutions per minute—the number of turns in one minute
s	seconds—unit of time
V6	V-shaped engine with six cylinders (three on each side of the "V")
V8	V-shaped engine with eight cylinders (four on each side of the "V")
V12	V-shaped engine with 12 cylinders (six on each side of the "V")
W16	W-shaped engine with 16 cylinders (four on each arm of the "W")

ALL ABOUT TIRES

Tires have codes that explain their sizes, and these codes are usually printed on the edge of each tire. As an example, a tire might have a code like **205/50 R15.**

205	means that the tire is 205 mm wide.
50	means that the "profile" (thickness, or height) of the tire is 50 percent of its width. The smaller the number, the thinner the tire.
R	means that the tire is a "radial"-type tire—it is made from layers of material that run in layers at right angles to the direction in which the tire rolls.
15	means that the tire is designed to fit on a 15-in-diameter wheel.

ARIEL ATOM 500

Huge power in a stripped-down two-seater for a true racing-car ride

- Only 25 Atom 500s have been built, all made specially to order for their owners.
- The car's gearbox allows full-throttle gear changes for incredible acceleration.
- The car has adjustable traction control and launch control systems.
- Each Atom 500 has an LCD instrument panel that includes a gearshift light.

The two-seater Ariel Atom first appeared in 2000 and is built by the same company that builds Ariel motorcycles. Most models have been built with Honda engines, either normally aspirated, supercharged, or turbocharged. All Atoms are superfast, but in 2010 Ariel decided to build a model with a 500-bhp V8 engine, which allowed for major performance!

The Atom looks more like a racing car than a road car, with an exposed tubular-steel chassis. The only body panels are the floor, nose, engine cover, and small mudguards over the wheels. If it rains, the driver needs a waterproof suit. A helmet is essential in any weather. The Atom 500, with its V8 engine, can be recognized from its big racing-car style rear wing and the small pods on the sides of the chassis housing the cooling radiators. The V8 engine was originally built by joining two Suzuki motorcycle engines together, though the final version was built specially for the Atom 500. Driving an Atom is more like riding a motorcycle than driving a car.

STATISTICS ARIEL ATOM 500

Price (new)	$200,000
Max speed	170 mph (274 kph)
0–62 mph (0–100 kph)	2.3 s
Engine type	V8 32-valve, normally aspirated
Engine capacity	3,000 cc
Max power	500 bhp (373 kW) at 10,600 rpm
Max torque	385 Nm (284 lb ft) at 7,750 rpm
Transmission	6-speed sequential gearbox, limited-slip differential
Suspension	Double wishbones front and rear with adjustable pushrod-operated spring/damper units
Wheels and tires	15-in front wheels; 16-in rear wheels; 205/50 R15 front tires; 245/45 R16 rear tires
Curb weight	1,212 lb (550 kg)
Length	145.5 in (3,696 mm)
Width	72.8 in (1,849 mm)
Height	47 in (1,194 mm)
Year introduced	2010

A BUGATTI VEYRON IS HEAVIER THAN THREE ATOM 500s!

BAC MONO

A race-inspired single-seater for the ultimate driving experience

- Options include a carbon crash helmet and made-to-order Mono racing suit pack.
- The sequential gearbox takes 35 milliseconds to complete a gear change.
- The Mono's cockpit controls include a touch-sensitive engine starter button.
- The leather interior trim is specially waterproofed.

In 2009, brothers Neill and Ian Briggs founded BAC (Briggs Automotive Company) to produce the Mono—a very lightweight, high-tech, single-seater sports car with stunning performance. The central driving position is designed to make the driver feel part of the car, and the seat and pedal positions are customized for each owner. It has no in-car entertainment, air conditioning, or satnav, though.

The car is built using carbon fiber over a steel safety cell, with a carbon-fiber nose section providing a small storage compartment and front crash protection. The body panels are designed to expose the Mono's mechanical components to reinforce the racing-car styling and to provide cooling air to the car's engine and radiators. Other features inspired by racing-car technology include the fully adjustable suspension five-point racing harness, detachable steering wheel, and adjustable pedals. For owners hoping to take their cars on the track, options include a carbon-ceramic brake kit, track-specific gear sets, lightweight exhaust system, and carbon wheel rims.

STATISTICS BAC MONO

Price (new)	$212,000
Max speed	170 mph (274 kph)
0–60 mph (0–97 kph)	2.8 s
Engine type	Mountune-developed, normally aspirated 4-cylinder, with double-overhead camshafts, variable valve timing
Engine capacity	2,488 cc
Max power	305 bhp (227 kW) at 8,000 rpm
Max torque	308 Nm (227 lb ft)
Transmission	6-speed Formula-3-specification sequential gearbox with limited-slip differential
Suspension	Double wishbones front and rear with bellcranks and pushrod-activated spring/damper units, rising rate and adjustable camber
Wheels and tires	17-in front and rear wheels; 205/40 R17 front tires; 245/40 R17 rear tires
Curb weight	1,279 lb (580 kg)
Length	155.6 in (3,952 mm)
Width	72.3 in (1,836 mm)
Height	43.7 in (1,110 mm)
Year introduced	2011

THE CAR HAS NO WINDSCREEN, SO A CRASH HELMET IS ESSENTIAL!

CAPARO T1

As close as you can get to a road-legal F1 car, with performance to matc

- A T1 was painted in police colors as a futuristic Rapid Response Vehicle!
- A small "aeroscreen" or a bubble canopy, like on a fighter plane, can be fitted to it.
- A magazine road-tester managed 0–100 mph (0–161 kph) in 6.2 s in a T1.
- Production stopped in 2015, but the car is due to be relaunched as the T1 Evo.

The T1 was originally called the Freestream T1, but the project was bought by the Caparo Vehicle Technologies company and renamed before it went into production in 2007. The car was designed by two engineers who worked on the McLaren F1 road-car project. They decided to produce a car that was as close as possible to a road-legal F1 racing car.

The engine is a 3.5-liter V8 that is based on a detuned IndyCar racing engine, and a carbon-fiber and aluminum-honeycomb monocoque chassis is used for the body. The car has a ground-effect rear diffuser like an F1 car, and the front and rear wings are adjustable to tune the aerodynamics. To complete the racing-car features, a quick-release steering wheel is provided, along with racing harnesses for the driver and passenger and a data-logging system. The car is a two-seater, with side-by-side seats, but the passenger sits slightly farther back than the driver so that their shoulders overlap, which means that the car can be narrower.

STATISTICS CAPARO T1

Price (new)	$300,000
Max speed	205 mph (330 kph)
0–62 mph (0–100 kph)	2.5 s
Engine type	Normally aspirated V8
Engine capacity	3,496 cc
Max power	575 bhp (429 kW) at 10,500 rpm
Max torque	420 Nm (310 lb ft) at 9,000 rpm
Transmission	6-speed sequential gearbox, limited-slip differential
Suspension	Double wishbones front and rear with adjustable racing spring/damper units
Wheels and tires	18-in front wheels; 19-in rear wheels; 235/40 R18 front tires; 295/30 R19 rear tires
Curb weight	1,036 lb (470 kg)
Length	160.1 in (4,066 mm)
Width	78.3 in (1,990 mm)
Height	42.4 in (1,076 mm)
Year introduced	2007

JUST 16 CAPARO T1s WERE EVER BUILT!

FERRARI FXX-K EVO

Ferrari's hybrid-powered "XX" car; technology for the future

- All "XX" cars are kept by Ferrari—owners can't take them home.
- An active rear spoiler lifts to slow the car under braking.
- The EVO produces 1,830 lb (830 kg) of downforce at the car's top speed.
- Engineers collect data from the cars' track sessions for use in future Ferraris.

The FXX-K, built between 2015 and 2017, is based on the car that was designed to be the ultimate Ferrari—the LaFerrari that translates to *The* Ferrari in English. Obviously, Ferrari decided that it wasn't "ultimate" enough! The FXX-K was Ferrari's first hybrid car, powered by a 6,262-cc V12 engine coupled to a HY-KERS hybrid system, giving a total power of 950 bhp (708 kW).

The FXX-K is a track-only car, which is part of Ferrari's "XX" track-day program. Ferrari produced 40 FXX-Ks, each car costing an estimated $2 million! In late 2017, Ferrari announced a special upgrade "EVO" aerodynamic package for the FXX-K, which increases the car's downforce by a huge 23 percent (while also reducing the weight of the car) thanks to revised bodywork and a full-size rear wing. The EVO also has special tire-monitoring sensors that record how the tires interact with the track as well as their temperatures and pressures. The FXX-K EVO is quicker on the track than many racing cars and sounds incredible!

STATISTICS FERRARI FXX-K EVO

Price (new)	$2.6 million
Max speed	217 mph (349 kph)
0–60 mph (0–97 kph)	2.5 s (estimate)
Engine type	Normally aspirated V12 internal combustion engine, plus HY-KERS electric motor
Engine capacity	6,262 cc
Max power	860 bhp (641 kW) at 9,200 rpm for V12 engine, plus 187 bhp (140 kW) from HY-KERS system, giving a total of 1,047 bhp (781 kW)
Max torque	750 Nm (553 lb ft) at 6,500 rpm from internal combustion engine, total torque including HY-KERS over 900 Nm (664 lb ft)
Transmission	7-speed dual-clutch gearbox, with electronic differential
Suspension	Front double wishbones, rear multi-link, with "magnetorheological" damping
Wheels and tires	19-in front wheels; 20-in rear wheels; 285/650 R19 front tires; 345/725 R20 rear tires
Curb weight	3,097 lb (1,405 kg)
Length	192.8 in (4,896 mm)
Width	80.7 in (2,051 mm)
Height	43.9 in (1,116 mm)
Year introduced	2015

THIS CAR WAS EVEN MORE POWERFUL THAN FERRARI'S F1 CAR.

McLAREN SENNA

A worthy tribute to a legendary F1 driver

- Named after three-time World Champion McLaren F1 driver Ayrton Senna.
- The monocoque chassis and bodywork are made from carbon fiber.
- Special black paint is used to reduce the amount of liquid used, saving weight!
- The aerodynamics produce 1,764 lb (800 kg) of downforce at 155 mph (249 kph).

The McLaren Senna is a sensational track-focused car. It is technically road-legal, but it is not aimed at road use. The only luggage space is a small storage area for two race suits and helmets, so no space for shopping or sports gear. It does, however, have a power-operated drink system to keep the driver hydrated!

McLaren's engineers designed this awesome machine to deliver the most intense driving experience of any McLaren road car. They did this by saving weight in every possible area of the car—including hollow carbon-fiber seats and even special lightweight paint! The RaceActive Chassis Control system has a race mode that lowers the car's ride height, increasing aerodynamic downforce and stiffening the suspension as the speed increases to cope with the high downforce loads. The system also controls the front and rear spoilers to stabilize the car and provide maximum grip. The car has a data-logging system to record each track lap, and optional extras include six-point racing harnesses for the driver and passenger.

STATISTICS MCLAREN SENNA

Price (new)	$1 million
Max speed	208 mph (335 kph)
0–62 mph (0–100 kph)	2.8 s
Engine type	Twin-turbo, alloy 32-valve V8 with twin electrically actuated twin-scroll turbochargers, double-overhead camshafts, variable valve timing
Engine capacity	3,994 cc
Max power	789 bhp (588 kW) at 7,250 rpm
Max torque	800 Nm (590 lb ft) at 5,500–6,700 rpm
Transmission	7-speed Seamless Shift Gearbox (SSG) with open differential and Brake Steer
Suspension	Double wishbones front and rear with active dampers and RaceActive Chassis Control II system
Wheels and tires	19-in front wheels; 20-in rear wheels; 245/35 R19 front tires; 315/30 R20 rear tires
Curb weight	2,886 lb (1,309 kg)
Length	186.8 in (4,744 mm)
Width	84.8 in (2,153 mm)
Height	47 in (1,195 mm)
Year introduced	2018

THE FOUR CARBON BRAKE DISCS TAKE SEVEN MONTHS EACH TO MANUFACTURE.

ULTIMA RS

A "build-it-yourself" Le Mans-style car with incredible performance

- Options include a rearview camera and parking sensors.
- The RS can brake from 100 mph (160 kph) to a standstill in an amazing 3.3 s!
- Two Ultimas were used as development cars for the McLaren F1 road car.
- For a race-car driving experience, no ABS or traction control is fitted.

The British-built Ultima RS was announced in June 2019 and is the fastest and most advanced Ultima so far. It is powered by a Chevrolet V8 engine and is available with several different power outputs, from a "basic" 480 bhp (358 kW) to an incredible 1,200 bhp (895 kW) for the top-of-the-range supercharged version!

The very first Ultima Mk1 was built in 1983 and was a mid-engined kit-car designed to look like a Le Mans car. It used donor parts from other cars, including Ford and Renault suspension, steering and brake parts, and a Renault engine and gearbox. Since that first car, Ultimas have been constantly updated and improved, and the company now makes all its own components, apart from the engine and gearbox. The most powerful version of the RS is a genuine hypercar and is capable of stunning performance with its 1,200-bhp (895 kW) Chevrolet V8. The RS has air conditioning, in-car entertainment, a digital dashboard with data logging, and an Ultima RS-branded set of luggage, plus optional gear to lift the front suspension for speed bumps!

STATISTICS ULTIMA RS

Price (new)	$120,000
Max speed	250 mph+ (402 kph+)
0–60 mph (0–97 kph)	2.3 s
Engine type	Supercharged Chevrolet V8
Engine capacity	6.2 liters
Max power	1,200 bhp (895 kW)
Max torque	969 Nm (715 lb ft) at 4,400 rpm
Transmission	Porsche 6-speed manual
Suspension	Double wishbones front and rear with coil spring/ damper units
Wheels and tires	19-in front and rear wheels; 265/30 R19 front tires; 325/30 R19 rear tires
Curb weight	2,050 lb (930 kg)
Length	164.2 in (4,170 mm)
Width	74.8 in (1,900 mm)
Height	44.3 in (1,125 mm)
Year introduced	2019

CARS CAN BE ORDERED FOR SELF-ASSEMBLY OR FULLY BUILT BY THE FACTORY.

GLOSSARY

camber: the inward or outward angle of the front tires on a car

chassis: steel tubes that carry the engine, seats, and other parts of a car

dampers: devices in a suspension system that prevent bouncing

differential: a set of gears that transmits engine power to the wheels and allow them to turn at different speeds on turns

hypercar: the most superior and high-performance car on the market

magnetorheological: having to do with a fluid controlled by a magnetic field, usually using an electromagnet

monocoque: a type of vehicle structure in which the body is combined with the chassis as a single unit

normally aspirated: describing an internal combustion engine in which air intake depends only on atmospheric pressure

supercharged: having to do with a device that increases the pressure of the fuel-air mixture in an internal combustion engine to achieve greater efficiency

suspension: a system of springs and other devices on a car that reduces the shaking and bumping caused by uneven surfaces

torque: a rotating force produced by an engine's crankshaft

transmission: the gear that transmits power from a car or truck's engine to the wheels

FOR MORE INFO

BOOKS

Goldsworthy, Steve. *The Tech Behind Race Cars*. North Mankato, MN: Capstone Press, 2020.

Skinner, Adam. *Fast Forward: The World's Most Famous Race Tracks and Race Cars*. Minneapolis, MN: Wide Eyed Editions, 2019.

West, David. *Race Cars*. Mankato, MN: Smart Apple Media, 2017.

WEBSITES

How Formula One Works
auto.howstuffworks.com/auto-racing/motorsports/formula-one2.htm
Read about this celebrated car race, including the special cars on the track.

McLaren
www.mclaren.com
Check out this legendary automaker's official site.

Race Cars
www.dkfindout.com/us/transportation/history-cars/race-cars/
Learn a bit about the history of racing and race cars.

Publisher's note to parents and teachers: Our editors have reviewed the websites listed here to make sure they're suitable for students. However, websites may change frequently. Please note that students should always be supervised when they access the internet.

INDEX